AMUSEMENT PARKS

Roller Coasters, Ferris Wheels, and Cotton Candy

By

JUDY ALTER

A First Book

Franklin Watts

New York London Hong Kong Sydney
Danbury, Connecticut

Photographs ©: Archive Photos: 9, 24, 30, 34; Cedar Point Image Library: chapter open-ers, 32, 57 (Dan Feicht); Corbis-Bettmann: 1, 11, 23, 26, 27 top; Culver Pictures: 7, 10, 14, 16, 27 bottom, 31; Dorney Park & Wildwater Kingdom: 54; Gamma-Liaison: 28 (John Brooks), 35; Gaylord Entertainment: 43 (Donnie Beauchamp); The Image Works: 52 bottom (F.J. Dean), 4 (Fujifotos), 47, 48 (John Griffin), 51 (Louise Gubb), 52 top (Lee Snider); Museum of the City of New York: 19, 21, 22; North Wind Picture Archives: 6; Photo Researchers: 45 (Mary Ann Hemphill), 38, 39 (Joyce Photographics), 44 (Richard T. Nowitz); Primadonna Casino Resorts: cover, 56; Sea World Inc.: 58, 42 (Ken Bohn); Superstock, Inc.: 49, 53; UPI/Corbis-Bettmann: 17, 37.

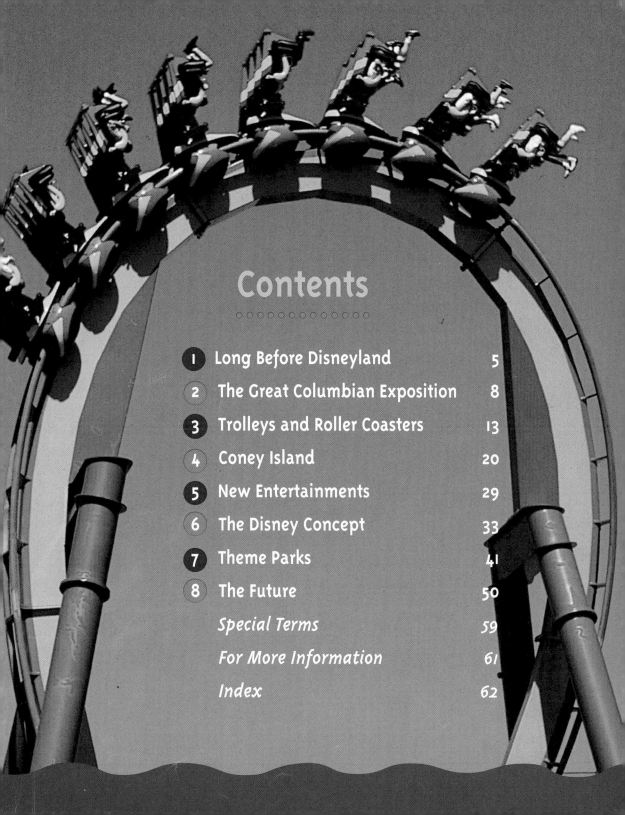

Contents

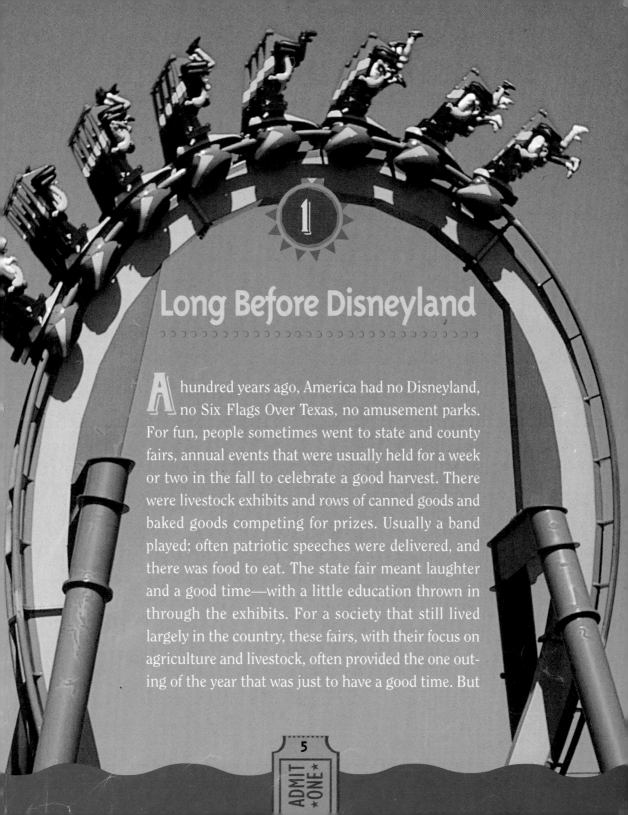

Long Before Disneyland

A hundred years ago, America had no Disneyland, no Six Flags Over Texas, no amusement parks. For fun, people sometimes went to state and county fairs, annual events that were usually held for a week or two in the fall to celebrate a good harvest. There were livestock exhibits and rows of canned goods and baked goods competing for prizes. Usually a band played; often patriotic speeches were delivered, and there was food to eat. The state fair meant laughter and a good time—with a little education thrown in through the exhibits. For a society that still lived largely in the country, these fairs, with their focus on agriculture and livestock, often provided the one outing of the year that was just to have a good time. But

ADMIT ONE

The New Hampshire State Fair, 1850s

as more people moved to the cities, they found the fairs less interesting. City dwellers didn't want to look at prize cattle or compare types of seed corn.

Amusement parks—enclosed areas designed for families to spend the day in recreation—began because people who lived in the cities wanted someplace to go for fun. Some people say that state and county fairs were the inspiration for amusement parks; others trace their roots all the way back to the trade fairs held in England in the Middle Ages. Both are right to some measure, but the real inspiration for the amusement park industry was the World's Columbian **Exposition** in Chicago in 1893.

A medieval market fair

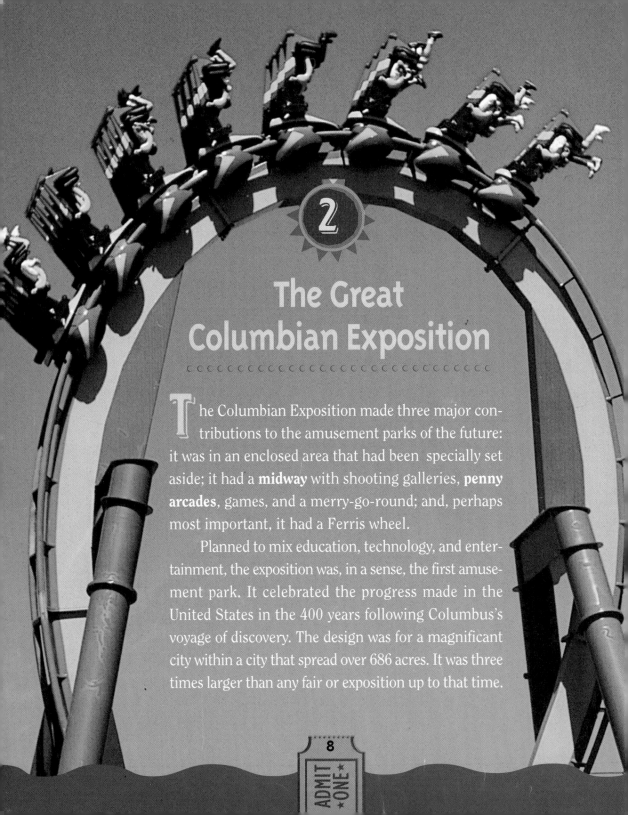

2

The Great Columbian Exposition

The Columbian Exposition made three major contributions to the amusement parks of the future: it was in an enclosed area that had been specially set aside; it had a **midway** with shooting galleries, **penny arcades**, games, and a merry-go-round; and, perhaps most important, it had a Ferris wheel.

Planned to mix education, technology, and entertainment, the exposition was, in a sense, the first amusement park. It celebrated the progress made in the United States in the 400 years following Columbus's voyage of discovery. The design was for a magnificant city within a city that spread over 686 acres. It was three times larger than any fair or exposition up to that time.

A panoramic view of the World's
Columbian Exposition, Chicago, 1893

Its major exhibition buildings were gleaming white, resembling Greek classical temples, with beautiful statues. There was a Machinery Building, larger than the Capitol in Washington, D.C.; the Manufactures and Liberal Arts Building, which was said to be the largest enclosed building constructed to that time; and buildings to show off mines and mining, agriculture, electricity, and other endeavors.

The Paris Exposition of 1889 had introduced **concessions**— spaces rented to salespeople or entertainers. Today concessions sell cotton candy or other food, offer games of chance like ring toss, or exhibit everything from sword swallowers to piano-playing chickens. The concessions made money but were considered "vulgar amusements." At the Columbian Exposition, concessions were kept apart from the exhibits. They were located in an entertainment area called the Midway Plaisance, a strip about a mile long. Many visitors compared the Midway Plaisance to a circus, and one newspaper

The Midway Plaisance at the Columbian Exposition

renamed it the "Royal Road of Gaiety." It featured restaurants, reproductions of villages from countries around the world—Germany, Egypt, Iceland, and others—shooting galleries and games of chance where people purchased tickets to shoot at fake ducks or targets or tried their luck in other ways. There was a great contrast between the main area of the exposition—with its elegant white buildings ablaze with thousands of lights and gentle music floating in the air— and the noisy street of the midway, with its enormous crowds.

The area in Chicago where the plaisance was located is still called the Midway today, but every amusement area at carnivals, circuses, and rodeos throughout the country is now also called a midway.

The most important attraction on the Midway was the Ferris wheel. Its inventor was George Washington Gale Ferris, who had been inspired by the paddle wheel in the coal mining community where he was raised. Standing 264 feet above the Midway, the wheel

The Ferris wheel at the Columbian Exposition

was the first machine to be developed from mechanical technology that was specifically designed to entertain—and scare—people.

When the wheel was first opened on June 21, 1893, it attracted larger crowds than ever before to the Midway. For fifty cents, a person could ride for twenty minutes, and although there was an outcry about the high price—ten times as much as it cost to ride the merry-go-round—more than a million people paid their money to try out the new contraption. Profits from the entire exposition were slim and any money made was probably due mostly to the Ferris wheel.

But the Columbian Exposition was temporary. Opened on May 1, 1893, its gates were closed permanently six months later. The fate of the first Ferris wheel after that closing was not a happy one. It was taken down and stored. Ferris finally opened a small park in Chicago to house his invention, but neighbors objected and Ferris went bankrupt. His wheel was sold at auction to a junk dealer who paid $1,800 for it. Riders enjoyed the original wheel one more time—at the Louisiana Purchase Exposition in Saint Louis in 1904. When that exposition closed, the wheel was not moved and became a rusting eyesore. It was destroyed by dynamite in 1906. Ferris, however, did not have to see the event: he had died in 1896.

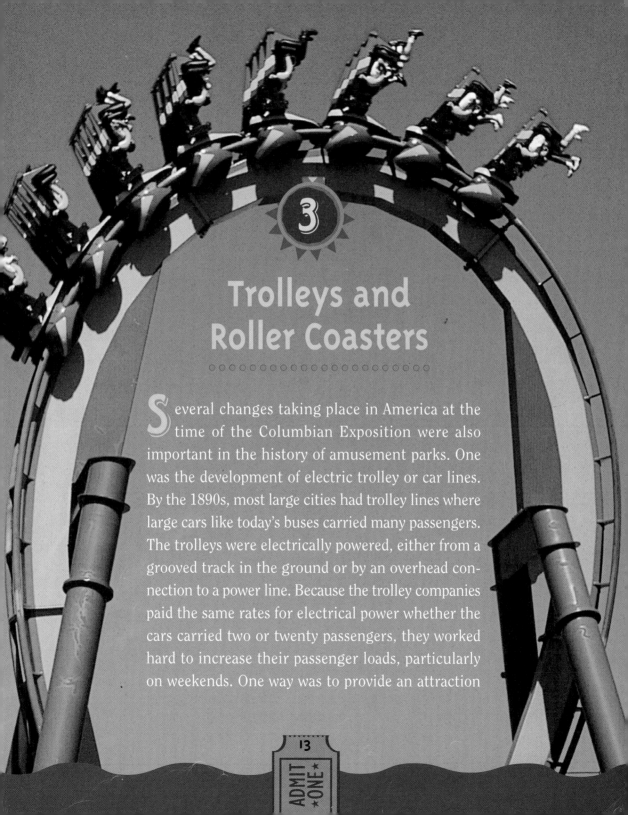

3

Trolleys and Roller Coasters

○○○○○○○○○○○○○○○○○○○○○○○○○○

Several changes taking place in America at the time of the Columbian Exposition were also important in the history of amusement parks. One was the development of electric trolley or car lines. By the 1890s, most large cities had trolley lines where large cars like today's buses carried many passengers. The trolleys were electrically powered, either from a grooved track in the ground or by an overhead connection to a power line. Because the trolley companies paid the same rates for electrical power whether the cars carried two or twenty passengers, they worked hard to increase their passenger loads, particularly on weekends. One way was to provide an attraction

A holiday crowd boards an electric trolley car
for a trip to Coney Island, 1895.

at the far end of the line—something that would encourage people
to spend their recreation time and money riding the trolley because,
in the day of open-air trolleys, getting there was half the fun. At
first companies created picnic areas, perhaps near a small lake or a
pleasant grove of trees. Gradually they added entertainments—

mechanical amusements such as a small Ferris wheel or a merry-go-round, dance halls, sports fields, restaurants. By 1919 there were between 1,500 and 2,000 amusement parks in the country, and most of them were owned by trolley companies.

At the time of the Columbian Exposition growing numbers of people lived in cities and worked in factories and businesses. People who had worked seven days a week on the farm now had a half day Saturday and all day Sunday to themselves. For the first time for many Americans, there was time and money for recreation.

One of the most important developments for the amusement park—more important than the Ferris wheel—was the **roller coaster**. While it did not reach its peak of popularity until the 1920s, the roller coaster—or the idea of it—had been quietly developing throughout much of the nineteenth century. The roller coaster, more than anything else, is the symbol of the amusement park industry. The curving lines of a roller coaster seem to suggest fun and freedom, in contrast to the serious and businesslike look of straight lines. Similarly, riding a roller coaster is a bit like being launched into space, in contrast to a ride on the merry-go-round, which is flatly rooted to earth. Roller coasters offer passengers exciting speed and the appearance of danger—while actually providing safety. Combining the two elements has been a challenge for inventors and designers.

Roller coasters can be traced back to early nineteenth-century Russian "sledders." For a fee, citizens could ride sleds down icy hills so steep that a guide had to accompany each rider, holding the rider

An early roller coaster, at Coney Island in 1904

in his lap for safety. The drawback to the adventure was that the sled then had to be lugged all the way back up the hill by hand.

The first artificial ride was built in Paris in 1804 and named the Russian Mountain. A carriage ran on a track that went down an artificial mountain. Unfortunately, the Russian Mountain had a high accident rate because of the steep angle of the incline and

The roller coaster
tracks curve,
suggesting fun
and adventure.

the high speed of the descent. Guard rails were added to keep the carriage from jumping the track.

Early American roller coasters were like **switchback railways**, in which the tracks zigzagged down mountains, creating a series of hairpin curves. But the coasters could not return passengers to the starting point. This meant the passengers had to walk back uphill.

In 1878, an inventor named Richard Knudson developed plans for an **inclined plane railway** that consisted of two wavy parallel tracks, with a lifting device at each end that raised the car and sent it back to the starting point. The idea was finally put into practice at New York's Coney Island in 1884 with Thompson's Switchback Railway. Cars held ten passengers who rode for a nickel each. Thompson took in $600 a day and recovered the money he had invested in three weeks.

At the same time and place, an inventor named Charles Alcoke developed an oval coaster track that returned passengers to their starting point. This was a major development in the history of roller coasters. Phillip Hinckle then developed a chain elevator system to pull loaded cars up an incline. These developments made possible roller coasters as we know them today.

The Roaring Twenties were the heyday of the great roller coasters—the Cyclone at New York's Coney Island, the Bobs at Riverview Park in Chicago, the Aero Coaster at Playland in Rye Beach, New York, and others.

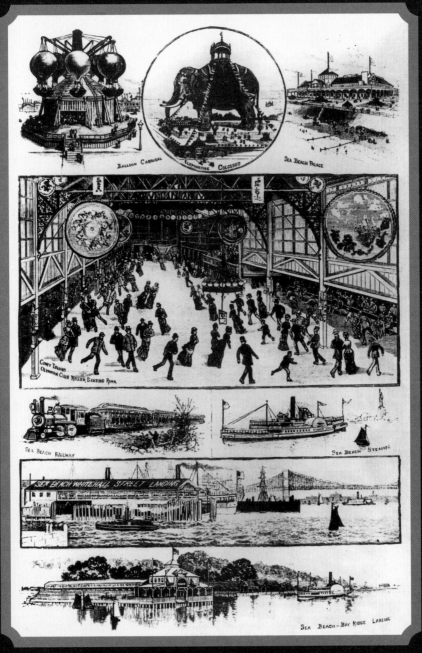

An old poster shows the variety of amusements the parks offered.

4

Coney Island

○○○○○○○○○○○○○○○○○○○○○○○

From the Columbian Exposition until Disneyland, Coney Island was "the" amusement park in America. Although many think that Coney Island is an actual park, it began instead as a place that was home to several enclosed parks, hotels, restaurants, and bathhouses.

In the mid-nineteenth century Coney Island was a beach wilderness at the foot of Brooklyn. By 1850, residents of New York City could travel out there in a horse-drawn streetcar. In the 1870s steamers offered a two-hour trip by water for fifty cents; in 1875, a railroad took passengers to Coney for thirty-five cents. In that first year, one million people rode the railroad; in the second year, two million. Then came the hotels

ADMIT ONE ★

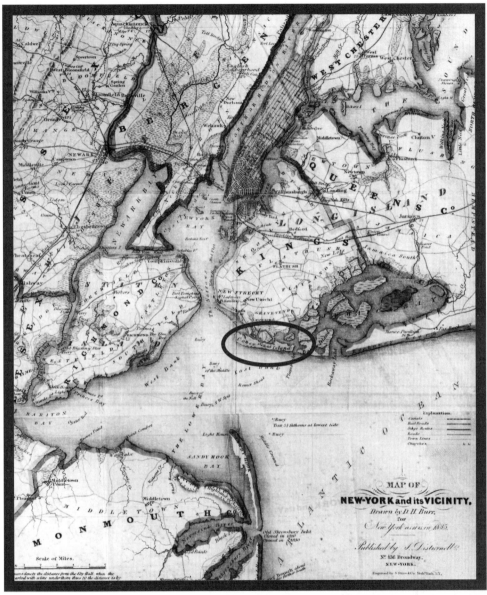

An 1835 map of the New York area shows Coney Island,
situated south of Brooklyn (Kings County).

A 1912 photograph shows Sunday arrivals at the trolley depot at Coney Island, ready for a day at the amusement park.

and amusement parks. By the late 1930s, twenty-five million people were visiting Coney Island during its five-month season.

Like many American cities, New York City was growing at an amazing rate. Many of the new residents of the city were between fifteen and thirty, and most had moved to the city from the country. Because they were young and had uprooted themselves, they were people who looked for excitement, thrills, even the sensation of danger. Coney Island was the perfect place for them to spend their free time and extra money, if they had any.

The early Coney Island included three major, privately owned parks, each distinctly different from the others. **Steeplechase** Park was the development of George Tilyou, a Coney Island native who invented the "one price" ticket. Once visitors paid the park entrance fee they could try all of his many rides and games—distorting mirrors, the Human Roulette Wheel, and the Whirlpool. Most of these devices were designed to throw strangers up against each other, cre-

A souvenir photo postcard shows the entrance to Steeplechase Park.

The Parachute Drop, one of the most famous Steeplechase amusements

ating a sensation of loss of control of one's own actions. The visitors tried amusements like the Blowhole, which sent blasts of air upward, raising skirts of unsuspecting women; and the Human Pool Table, which threw people in several directions, causing them to lose control of their limbs. While enjoying the amusements, the visitors became entertainment for others who were watching.

Visitors to Luna Park escaped their everyday lives in a fantasyland of bright lights and never-ending motion. There were live entertainment shows, exotic cities, an American-Indian village, a re-creation of the canals of Venice, a Dutch windmill, and a Japanese garden. Fantasy rides took visitors under the sea and into space as far as the moon. It was all good, clean fun, and family entertainment.

The third park, Dreamland, tried to re-create the Columbian Exposition, with classical buildings and thousands of lights. The designers wanted a park with sophistication and educational value, and they offered gigantic productions such as "Fighting the Flames," which employed 4,000 characters, and the Lilliputian Village of 300 midgets. But visitors to Coney Island wanted noise and entertainment and fun, not culture and education, and Dreamland was a failure. Before it could close, it was destroyed in a spectacular fire.

Coney Island had a security problem. It not only attracted thrill-seeking, law-abiding citizens, but also drew gamblers and con men—criminals or shady characters who walked the edge of the law. Their presence at Coney Island cast a shadow over the entire amusement park industry, a blot that the industry still works hard to overcome by establishing an image of family entertainment. At Steeplechase

Elephant riding, a Luna Park attraction

and Luna parks, one reason for charging an admission fee was to keep out troublemakers.

Coney Island is still an amusement area today, recording an amazing 50 million visitors a year—although that figure probably includes repeated visits by nearby residents. A smaller park named Dreamland, after the original, opened in 1991, joining five other parks at the beach resort. True to the spirit of the first Coney Island amusement parks, it offered free admission, with low-cost rides— $1 for children's rides, and $2.50 for other rides, with the option of

LUNA PARK. SURF AVENUE. BY NIGHT, CONEY ISLAND. N. Y.

Souvenir postcards of Luna Park (top) and Dreamland

Coney Island today

a pay-one-price entrance fee of $10 . . . a reasonable outing for working families.

Coney Island is recognized as an important historical site that should be preserved. Although much of the original playland lies in ruins, the Cyclone roller coaster, once condemned, has been rebuilt and "Sideshows by the Seashore" features attractions such as a sword swallower, a bearded lady, and a woman who dances with a live python. The New York Aquarium is located at Coney Island, along with a theater company that presents plays using themes from the midway. And in summer, people walk the boardwalk, sit on the beach, and swim in the ocean. It's not what it once was, but Coney Island still draws the crowds.

5

New Entertainments

By the late 1920s, amusement parks were in trouble for several reasons. One was the increasing popularity of the automobile. As more and more people bought automobiles, they began to take longer trips and were no longer limited to finding amusement in their own neighborhoods or city. Most amusement parks were set in the midst of the city and had no room to expand and provide the needed parking spaces. Bad summer weather several years in a row also kept crowds away from the parks. Then came the stock market crash of 1929 and the Great Depression. Many people were out of work and had more serious things than amusement on their minds—like food for their tables.

In the 1940s and early 1950s, the parks faced new

During the Great Depression, a time of soup kitchens and food lines, amusement parks drew few visitors.

problems. In those years, large numbers of Americans moved to the suburbs to escape the problems of city living—overcrowding and crime—and to pursue the American dream. Safely settled in their suburban homes, American families clustered in the living room around a new invention—television. Being close to the city—once important for parks—turned into a disadvantage. Amusement parks were taken over by gangs of city youths. Fights were common, and racial differences were often a factor behind those fights. Parks grew so dangerous that the average family refused to attend them, or to let their children attend.

By the late 1950s, most amusement parks were gone. Many met a fate similar to that of Riverview Park in Chicago, which had been in operation since 1904 and was known as a testing ground for new rides. At the height of its popularity, Riverview had 25 major rides in addition to 11 roller coasters—including the Bobs, called the ultimate roller coaster, and the Fireball, which reached a then-astounding speed of 65 miles an hour. In 1967, the park and the equipment were sold, and the site was bulldozed to make room for a shopping center, parking, and factories.

One park that survived was Cedar Point, near Sandusky, Ohio.

Many of the early amusement parks were shut down.

Cedar Point, in Ohio, has grown from a small amusement park
to a large complex with many attractions.

Begun in 1870 as a Lake Erie bathhouse—complete with a water toboggan—the park is one of the oldest amusement parks in the country. It has kept up with the times and became a "complete resort destination" by adding such features as a water amusement area called Soak Park, hotel accommodations, and a Rock and Roll Hall of Fame and Museum.

In the 1950s, when Cedar Point was scheduled to be torn down, it was rescued by a group of Ohio businesspeople. They were inspired by Disneyland and the idea of a **theme park** that would offer family entertainment. In the 1990s Cedar Point was named the best amusement park in the world for three years in a row by readers of *Inside Track*, an international newspaper that regularly rates the amusement industry.

6

The Disney Concept

○○○○○○○○○○○○○○○○○○○○○○○○○○○○○○○○○○○

D isneyland Park, which opened July 17, 1955, changed the amusement industry forever by creating an organized "fantasy" world of pleasure. It combines the charm of an old-fashioned past with the latest technology to provide spectacular effects. In the offices of WED (Walter Elias Disney) Enterprises, it's called "**imagineering**"—a combination of imagination and engineering.

Walt Disney may be credited with one of the greatest creative imaginations of any twentieth-century American. His amusement parks—Disneyland, Walt Disney World Resort, and Epcot—were the crowning achievements of a long and distinguished career of providing wholesome family entertainment

Walt Disney World Resort and Epcot in Florida

for Americans. But nobody would have suspected the future when Disney was a youngster.

Walt Disney was born in Chicago in 1901, not many years after the Columbian Exposition. Probably he heard much about that great event from his parents and older brothers. The boy spent his childhood on a farm in Missouri, where his family struggled to avoid poverty. Later he was a newsboy in Kansas City for six years, sold food on railroad trains, was a mail carrier, and served with the American Red Cross in France just after World War I—all before he was eighteen. He was, at best, an ordinary student. His one talent—and interest—was cartooning. Then, through his work in advertising in Kansas City in the 1920s, he was introduced to **animation** in its early and crude days, and he found his artistic medium. His first company created animated cartoons— motion pictures consisting of a series of drawings, each only slightly different from the previous one. When run together at high speed through a motion picture projector, they gave the impression of movement by living characters. Unfortunately, the company went bankrupt.

Walt Disney, with his most famous creation, Mickey Mouse

Walt Disney arrived in Hollywood in 1923. Within months, he and his brother Roy had established the Disney Brothers Studio. His first successful creation was Mickey Mouse, based on a mouse he remembered from his Kansas City office but bearing, most said, a striking resemblance to Walt himself. *Steamboat Willie*, the first Mickey Mouse cartoon, appeared in 1928, followed by *Plane Crazy* and *The Gallopin' Gaucho*. His company and his work grew so rapidly that by 1937, when he produced his first animated success, *Snow White and the Seven Dwarfs*, Walt Disney had a staff of 750 people.

During World War II he made films for the government, but all the time he was imagining an amusement park, which he saw as an ever-growing, ever-changing project, unlike films which, once completed, could not be changed. Taking a lesson from the Columbian Exposition, he saw his parks as a world apart from everyday life. Planning began in 1952, and Disneyland opened on July 17, 1955. Its start was shaky, but then the magic land attracted over a million guests in its first six months and was self-supporting within a year.

Disneyland is actually many lands within one theme park. Guests enter through Main Street, a picture-perfect, old-time small town with a railroad station, city hall, ice cream parlor, firehouse, barber shop, movie house, drugstore, and so on. This single entrance to the park allows officials to control crowds and prevent some of the problems of fights and rowdy behavior that had occurred in amusement parks during the 1950s.

Beyond Main Street are four "lands": In Fantasyland, visitors ride on King Arthur's leaping horses, through the Sleeping Beauty

In 1988, Disney World celebrated Mickey Mouse's sixtieth anniversary by inviting 4,000 children from around the world to a grand parade and party in the park.

Fantasyland (top) and Frontierland

Tomorrowland

castle, on Peter Pan's flight to Never Never Land, into the Seven Dwarfs' diamond mine, or to Alice's Mad Tea Party. Frontierland offers Davy Crockett's stockade, stagecoaches rushing through the desert, Mississippi steamboats, and other nineteenth-century ways to travel. Adventureland takes guests on a jungle river ride, complete with such dangers as hippos charging the boat, cannibals dancing on the shore, hungry crocodiles, and threatening rapids and waterfalls. Tomorrowland gives visitors the sensation of being transported to the moon on a rocket.

Attractions in the "lands" have changed over the years, but much about Disneyland remains the same: it is well-landscaped so that everything, like Main Street, is picture perfect. Walkways are wide, so that visitors never feel crowded. The attractions are found at Disneyland only and are not seen at other amusement parks. Visitors find varieties of food—not just ballpark hot dogs and greasy nachos.

Disneyland is also kept extremely clean. When Disney first had the idea of the park, his wife asked why he wanted to build an amusement park. She said that such parks were "always so dirty." Disney is said to have answered, "That's just the point—mine won't be."

Critics have complained that Disneyland presents an unreal world where life is clean, bright, safe, and never challenging. They claim that Americans visiting Disneyland are once again couch potatoes—receiving their entertainment without actively reaching out for it, being acted upon instead of acting. Others have pointed out that the lands of Disneyland, particularly Main Street, U.S.A., feature no ethnic nor racial minorities and do not celebrate the many cultures that make up our country.

7

Theme Parks

Early imitators of Disneyland failed, but in 1961 the successful Six Flags Over Texas opened near Dallas, Texas, followed by Six Flags Over Georgia, near Atlanta, and Six Flags Over Mid-America, near Saint Louis, Missouri. These parks mixed historical settings with entertainment and featured big-name stars in live entertainment shows and exciting thrill rides—a log flume ride through rapids, a steel coaster with three back-to-back vertical loops, a parachute drop, another steel coaster that turns riders upside down six times. Other theme parks followed the success of the Six Flags idea—Silver Dollar City in Bransom, Missouri; Busch Gardens in Tampa, Florida, and Williamsburg, Virginia; the Sea World parks in San Antonio, Texas, San

Sea World offers entertainment, thrills, and education.

Diego, California, Cleveland, Ohio, and Orlando, Florida. Most of today's major amusement parks were built in the 1970s.

Successful theme parks in the last quarter of the twentieth century have recognized the importance of location: close enough to cities for families to get there easily, yet far enough beyond the city bus route to discourage rowdy youths. It takes a car to get to most parks, and that encourages family visits. These parks are also far enough out that they could be built on land that was not nearly as expensive as that closer to a big city.

Newer theme parks include Opryland in Nashville, Tennessee.

The most successful theme park to follow Disneyland was the Walt Disney World Resort in Florida, possibly the biggest tourist attraction in the United States. Walt Disney learned from his experience with Disneyland, especially the fact that it was built on too small a piece of property. The Disney corporation did not own enough land around it, and soon the park was surrounded by cheap motels and restaurants, all catering to visitors to the park. Disney wanted to correct that in his next project: the Walt Disney World Resort in central Florida, which would feature hotels and resorts; places for swim-

The plans for EPCOT center included this space pavilion,
to show the progress toward space travel.

ming, fishing, boating, and other recreational sports; along with the
exhibits and rides of an amusement park.

A central part of the new park was to be Disney's city of the
future, EPCOT (Experimental Prototype Community of Tomorrow),
which would have permanent residences, businesses, and schools.
Disney saw EPCOT, like the earlier Disneyland, as never completed,
always becoming. He also saw it as a possible answer to one of America's most serious responsibilities: finding solutions to the problems
of our cities, the same problems that caused the closing of many
amusement parks in the 1950s.

WED Enterprises purchased over 27,000 acres in Florida—an
area twice the size of Manhattan in New York City. By the mid-1990s,

only slightly over 5,000 acres were developed, leaving a secure safety zone around the attraction.

Phase I of the Walt Disney World Resort opened in October, 1971, but Walt Disney never saw his dream become reality: he died of lung cancer in 1966. Nonetheless his company, led by his older brother, Roy, fulfilled Walt's dream.

At its opening, the resort consisted of The Magic Kingdom—the major entertainment area which is entered by way of an old-fashioned Main Street; two resort hotels, the Contemporary Resort and the Polynesian Resort; and a small campground. Disney World not only

The Magic Kingdom

provided a unique entertainment experience, but it has also been seen as a model of city planning because of its rapid mass-transit system, its moving sidewalks, and its efficient sewage and power systems. It is truly a world unto itself.

It is the Magic Kingdom that draws millions of people annually. Bigger and better than Disneyland, it includes many of the familiar attractions—Frontierland, Adventureland, Fantasyland, and Tomorrowland—but the buildings are larger and taller and the sense of action is faster. Cinderella Castle, for instance, is much grander than Sleeping Beauty Castle in Disneyland. Although thrill rides were not a part of Disney's original plan, they have been added at both sites—perhaps to keep up with the competition.

One of the most interesting technical developments in the park is the use of AudioAnimatronics, a technique that creates three-dimensional characters whose voices and movements are controlled by computer electronics. The figures are built of plastic with a realistic vinyl-like skin, and they do seem to walk, talk, and follow you with their eyes. These characters explain exhibits at various points throughout the Magic Kingdom. This is but one example of the technology used to make fantasy seem real throughout the park.

Most visitors to Disney World are vacationers who can afford to fly or drive the distance to the park and put their family up for several days in a hotel. Few blue-collar workers are able to take advantage of its wonders—which puts Disney World a long distance from Coney Island, which attracted ordinary working people.

In 1975—nine years after Disney's death and four years after

AudioAnimatronic robots in an exhibit of prehistoric life

the opening of Walt Disney World—WED Enterprises announced that it was moving ahead with plans for EPCOT Center, to be called, Epcot. Opened in 1982, the center is not the futuristic city that its creator imagined. In the years following Disney's first vision of Epcot, the land and situation had changed, making it necessary to alter the original plans. There are no residential or industrial areas at Epcot; instead, one executive described the center as a permanent world's fair—a modern Columbian Exposition that will never close its gates.

Epcot consists of two main areas—Future World and World Showcase. The first shows off American accomplishments in technology, with buildings or pavilions for each major industry, as there were at the Columbian Exposition. Pavilions in Future World are created in cooperation with major corporations. For example, the World of Motion, sponsored by General Motors, emphasizes the importance of automobile ownership and displays advances in car design. Other buildings are devoted to computers, food processing, communications, and plastics. For the most part, these pavilions trace the history of developments, rather than predicting the future.

In World Showcase, the American pavilion is central. It surveys American history in a twenty-nine minute presentation narrated by Mark Twain and Benjamin Franklin, covering everything from the Civil War and slavery, the Plains Indian Wars, and the struggle for

An Epcot exhibit of industry

women's rights, to the Great Depression and the attack on Pearl Harbor at the start of World War II. Other pavilions represent France, Mexico, Canada, Japan, Italy, China, and other countries.

Critics complain that these exhibits are cleaned-up history, showing none of its problems. In the World of Motion's display of the development of the automobile, for instance, there is no mention of the problems of smog or gridlock or of highway accidents. In the World Showcase tour of American history, contemporary social problems—including recent wars—are not included. Walt Disney World, says one student of amusement parks, is the American version of paradise.

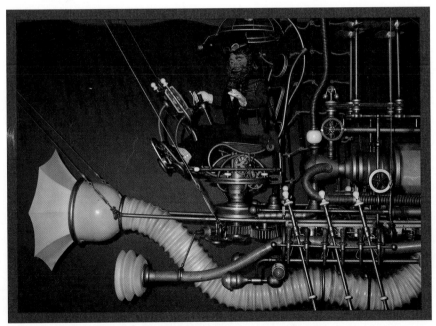

A flying machine in the AudioAnimatronic exhibit of the history of aviation

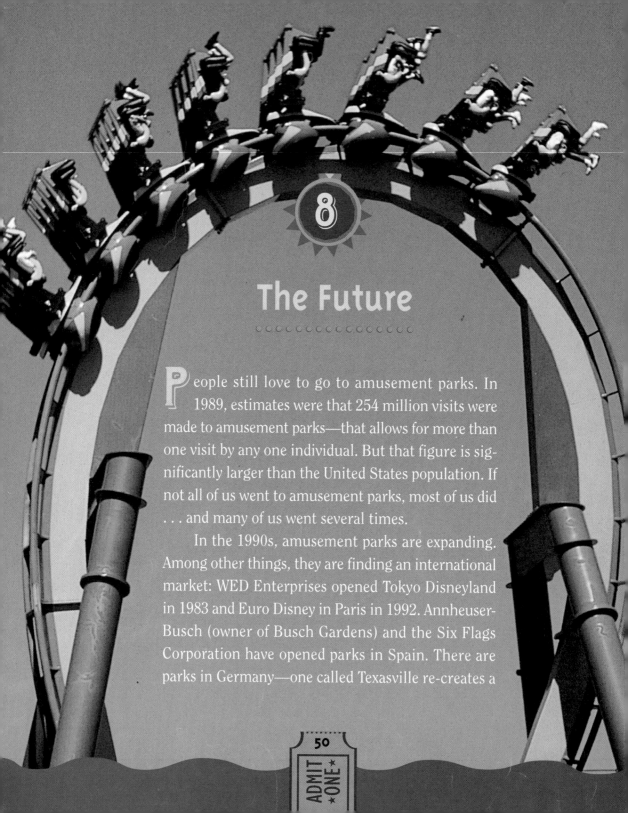

8

The Future

○○○○○○○○○○○○○○○○○○

People still love to go to amusement parks. In 1989, estimates were that 254 million visits were made to amusement parks—that allows for more than one visit by any one individual. But that figure is significantly larger than the United States population. If not all of us went to amusement parks, most of us did . . . and many of us went several times.

In the 1990s, amusement parks are expanding. Among other things, they are finding an international market: WED Enterprises opened Tokyo Disneyland in 1983 and Euro Disney in Paris in 1992. Annheuser-Busch (owner of Busch Gardens) and the Six Flags Corporation have opened parks in Spain. There are parks in Germany—one called Texasville re-creates a

An amusement park in South Africa

town in America's Old West. England boasts a good number of parks which are British in theme and, said one spokesperson for the British Tourist Authority, much preferred by English children. One, a stately castle and park, suddenly drew huge crowds when it introduced thrill rides. Denmark has Tivoli, one of Europe's oldest and largest parks, as well as the newer Legoland, where everything from buildings to thousands of art objects and pieces of miniature furniture are made of Lego building blocks. Australia boasts four parks—Sea World, Wet and Wild, Dream World, and Warner Brothers Movie World, although tourist officials claim that only the last is related to any American park, despite the name similarities.

Tivoli (top), a historic Danish amusement park, and the newer Legoland

An amusement park in a shopping mall in Alberta, Canada

Amusement parks in shopping malls are a new idea, blending traditional amusement park entertainments—roller coasters, water parks, carousels, and live entertainment performances—with hotels, movie theaters, and shopping facilities. Giant mall parks exist at West Edmonton Mall, Alberta, Canada; Ontario Palace, Toronto; Pier 39, San Francisco; Mall of America, Bloomington, Minnesota; and other locations.

But in spite of these new attractions, and although attendance grows steadily, fewer new parks are being built in the 1990s. This is

The White Cyclone, in Japan, and Hercules, in Pennsylvania, are among the highest wooden roller coasters in the world.

because they are so expensive—between $600 and $700 million—to build and to operate. Statistics are hard to come by, but parks generally must return at least 80 percent of their revenue into operating budget. For every dollar taken in, 80 cents goes toward operating the park.

Existing parks strive to outdo each other, by adding rides that are more and more thrilling. In the early 1990s, Dorney Park, in Pennsylvania, and Six Flags Over Texas almost went to court in a battle over who had the right to claim the highest wooden roller coaster in the world. Dorney Park claimed their new ride, Hercules, won with a drop of 157 feet. Six Flags Over Texas conceded that Hercules had a higher drop than their Texas Giant, with a drop of 137 feet. But, said a spokesperson, the structure of the Texas Giant stood at 143 feet, which was much higher than that of Hercules, which was built at the side of a hill and thereby gained an advantage. Does it matter? According to executives at both parks, being able to call their wooden coaster the highest in the world has international significance.

In the war of the wooden roller coasters, one old giant hangs on. Today's owner of Astroland at Coney Island has announced his determination to preserve the Cyclone, the famous coaster built in 1927, in spite of the high coast of keeping it repaired and in working order. The Cyclone is officially recognized as a New York landmark and is listed in a register of landmarks.

Nonetheless the older rides have been outdone. A roller coaster at a park called Buffalo Bill—a side attraction to a Nevada gambling casino—boasts the Desperado with a height of 220 feet and a higher speed than any other coaster. New in 1995 at OpryLand/Nashville was the Sky Coaster, where a person could be strapped into a harness, raised 152 feet into the air, and allowed to free-fall for 50 feet— in a sort of roller coaster without tracks. Six Flags Over Houston introduced an indoor roller coaster that operates in the dark—called, appropriately, a "dark thrill ride." And Cedar Point boasts that readers of *Inside Track* rated its ride, Magnum XL-200, the number-one roller coaster in the world for two years.

In the ongoing competition for new thrills, Six Flags Over Texas introduced The Right Stuff in 1995 . This Mach 1 Adventure is an aviation ride in which 100 riders at a time sit in two-passenger cockpits and are sent soaring through the clouds to burst through the

The Desperado, at Buffalo Bill Park

sound barrier. Universal City has recently offered Terminator II, a four-dimensional interactive experience in which people can combat Arnold Schwartzenegger. What next? Whatever the highly paid "imagineering" people of the various corporations can dream up.

Amusement park owners are also aware of the aging of America—

Magnum XL-200, at Cedar Point

more people are living longer in better health. Amusement parks now also have an older audience that wants less danger and speed; more restaurants, landscaping, and gardens; more live entertainment. This older population is expected to be particularly attracted to parks combined with shopping facilities.

Today's families are finding that a day at a big theme park is expensive. The regular admission often runs about $30 at many parks, with discounts for children and senior citizens. Parking adds from $6 to $10, and ticket prices do not include food, which can be costly. A family of four can easily spend $150 in one day at a park.

Amusement parks continue to offer new rides and new thrills to visitors.

Amusement parks will never be without their critics, in spite of their popularity. Some people claim that as parks strive to outdo each other with higher roller coasters, scarier rides, and more complicated technology, the kind of pleasure that gave rise to amusement parks is lost. The child who rides the Texas Giant and soars to the moon with the help of Virtual Reality may never appreciate the quiet pleasures of a picnic by the lake or a small county fair. Bigger, these critics say, is not necessarily better. The county fair, the Fourth of July picnic, the Sunday family outing by a lake are all a part of the American heritage that should not fade away.

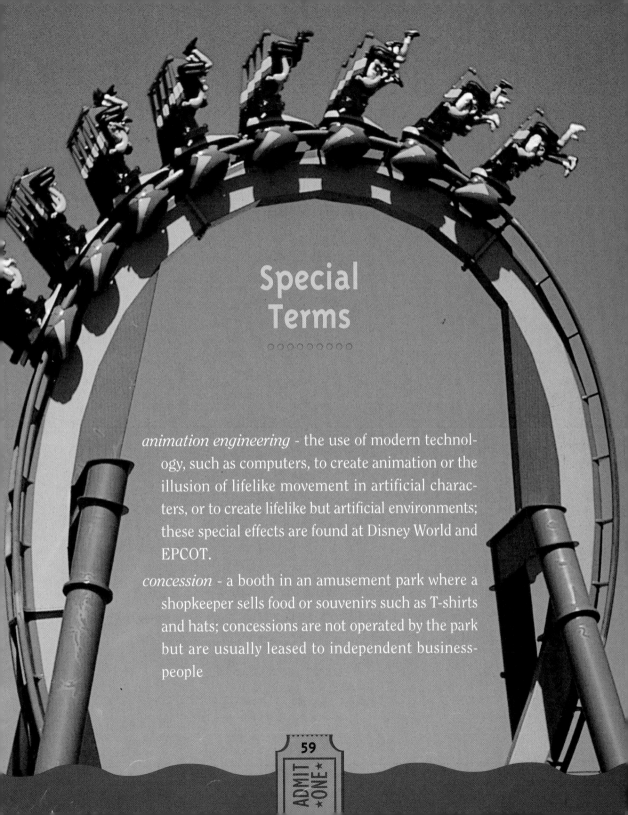

Special Terms

animation engineering - the use of modern technology, such as computers, to create animation or the illusion of lifelike movement in artificial characters, or to create lifelike but artificial environments; these special effects are found at Disney World and EPCOT.

concession - a booth in an amusement park where a shopkeeper sells food or souvenirs such as T-shirts and hats; concessions are not operated by the park but are usually leased to independent businesspeople

ADMIT ONE ★

exposition - an exhibit, often of specific products, such as an automobile exposition, an agricultural exposition, a livestock exposition

inclined plane railway - a railway that goes straight along an inclined or rising plane (as opposed to a switchback)

midway - the place at a fair where you find carnival-like amusements, such as games of chance, the Ferris wheel and other rides, and food

penny arcade - a hall or walkway in an amusement park with entertainment games, such as pinball machines. These once could be played for a penny; today they are still pretty cheap

roller coaster - a small railway of open cars that follows a specially built track of loops, curves, and high rises, so that passengers enjoy frightening bursts of speed and sudden plunges from great heights

steeplechase - a horse race on a dirt track, with hedges, ditches, and other obstacles that the horses must jump

switchback railway - a railway track that climbs a mountain by a series of zigzag curves, so that it goes across the face of the mountain in one direction at a slight rise, then switches and goes across in the other direction. With each switchback, the railway track climbs a little higher

theme park - an amusement park built around a certain theme or idea: Disney World or Disneyland, Six Flags Over Texas, Legoland in Denmark

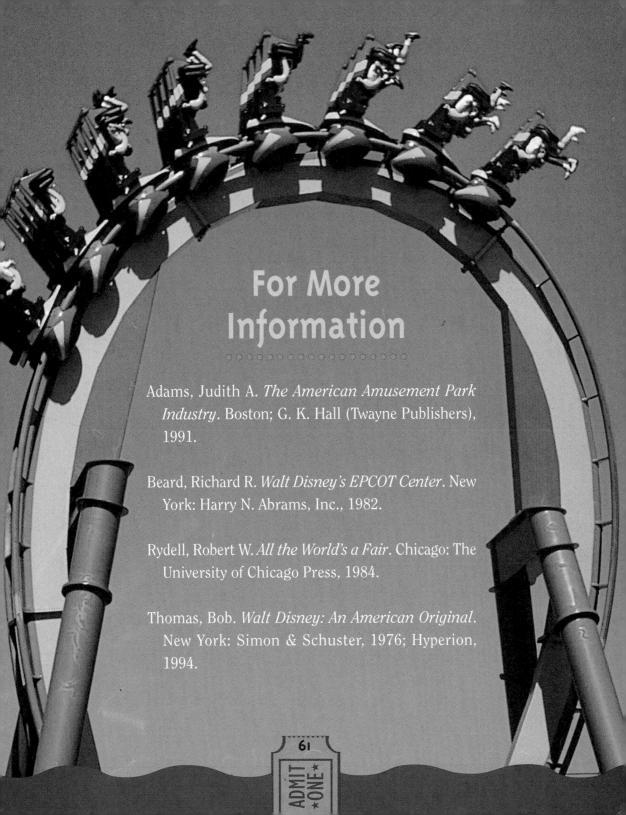

For More
Information

Adams, Judith A. *The American Amusement Park Industry*. Boston; G. K. Hall (Twayne Publishers), 1991.

Beard, Richard R. *Walt Disney's EPCOT Center*. New York: Harry N. Abrams, Inc., 1982.

Rydell, Robert W. *All the World's a Fair*. Chicago: The University of Chicago Press, 1984.

Thomas, Bob. *Walt Disney: An American Original*. New York: Simon & Schuster, 1976; Hyperion, 1994.

Index

ADMIT ONE ★